T0368569

Just Like Me

By Brittni C. Delaney Odang

Illustrated by Endra Andoyo

AuthorHouse™
1663 Liberty Drive
Bloomington, IN 47403
www.authorhouse.com
Phone: 1 (833) 262-8899

Because of the dynamic nature of the Internet, any web addresses or links contained in this book may have changed
since publication and may no longer be valid. The views expressed in this work are solely those of the author and do
not necessarily reflect the views of the publisher, and the publisher hereby disclaims any responsibility for them.

Any people depicted in stock imagery provided by Getty Images are models,
and such images are being used for illustrative purposes only.
Certain stock imagery © Getty Images.

Interior Image Credit: Endra Andoyo

ISBN: 978-1-6655-0501-7 (sc)
      978-1-6655-0500-0 (e)

Library of Congress Control Number: 2020921108

Published by AuthorHouse 10/23/2020

authorHOUSE®

For Lula, Jibryil & Alessa.

Thank you for inspiring me
and making my days brighter.

There has always
been a question
I could never
really answer.

A question that
always makes
me wonder...

"Are you more like Mommy or like Daddy?"

Mommy loves the city.

Daddy loves the country.

I think I'm just like my Daddy,

but I like the city too!

Mommy loves the color pink.

Daddy loves the color blue.

I think I'm just
like my Mommy,

but I like the color blue too!

Mommy loves to cook.

Daddy loves to eat.

I think I'm just like my Daddy,

but I like
cooking too!

Mommy loves to write.

Daddy loves to read.

I think I'm just like my Mommy,

but I like reading too!

Mommy loves to dance.

Daddy loves to sing.

I think I'm
just like
my Daddy,

but I like dancing too!

I'm just like Mommy,
but I'm also like Daddy...

Printed in the United States
By Bookmasters